Katie Lede

A Little Golden Book® Biography

By Shana Corey · Illustrated by Jen Bricking

🌸 A GOLDEN BOOK • NEW YORK

Text copyright © 2024 by Shana Corey
Cover art and interior illustrations copyright © 2024 by Jen Bricking
All rights reserved. Published in the United States by Golden Books, an imprint of Random
House Children's Books, a division of Penguin Random House LLC, 1745 Broadway,
New York, NY 10019. Golden Books, A Golden Book, A Little Golden Book, the G colophon,
and the distinctive gold spine are registered trademarks of Penguin Random House LLC.
rhcbooks.com
Educators and librarians, for a variety of teaching tools, visit us at RHTeachersLibrarians.com
Library of Congress Control Number: 2023945554
ISBN 978-0-593-70625-1 (trade) — ISBN 978-0-593-70626-8 (ebook)
Printed in the United States of America
10 9 8 7 6 5 4 3 2 1

D1524698

Katie Ledecky is one of the greatest swimmers of all time. She is a record setter, a world champion, and an Olympic gold medalist. Some people call her the greatest athlete in the world!

Katie was born Kathleen Genevieve Ledecky on March 17, 1997, in Washington, DC. She grew up in Bethesda, Maryland, with her mother, her father, and her big brother, Michael.

Swimming was important in Katie's family. When her mother was a little girl, her sister fell into the water on a vacation and almost drowned. After that, all the children in the family learned to swim.

When Katie's mom grew up, she taught her kids how to swim as well. Right from the start, Katie loved the water!

When Katie was six years old, she and her brother signed up for a summer swim league called the Palisades Porpoises. They liked it so much they were soon swimming and racing all year round.

From a young age, Katie loved a challenge. She'd write down goals for how fast she wanted to swim. Even if it seemed difficult at first, Katie kept trying until she reached her goal.

Katie was competitive—
in and out of the water.
She also enjoyed playing
basketball and soccer,
but swimming was
her favorite.

No matter what
the sport, Katie liked to
win. But that didn't stop
her from always being
a good teammate. She
cheered her friends'
successes as well as
her own.

Katie worked hard to be the best swimmer she could be! She woke up early to practice before school. Many days, she'd swim again after school, too.

Swimming uses a lot of energy. Katie ate peanut butter toast and a banana on the way to the pool and drank chocolate milk after practice to keep up her strength.

Katie's coach helped her learn a new stroke called the gallop or loping stroke. It's a freestyle technique where one arm strokes harder than the other. This style helped her swim even faster.

Katie kept practicing, and when she was in eighth grade, she set a new goal for herself—to make it to the Olympics!

It wasn't long before she achieved that goal. In the summer of 2012, Katie earned a spot on the US Olympic team! She headed to the Olympic Games in London, England. She was only fifteen years old, the youngest member of that year's US team.

Most people didn't expect Katie to win. But Katie didn't focus on what other people thought. She dove into the water and quickly took the lead. The crowd couldn't believe it! Katie not only won the Olympic gold medal for the women's 800-meter freestyle—she won by more than four seconds and broke the twenty-three-year-old US record!

Katie was an Olympic gold medalist. But she was still a high school student. When she wasn't swimming, she spent time with her family, did homework, and played board games.

She went to the movies with friends

and volunteered
to help others.

Over the next few years, Katie set record after record. She won long races and short races. And Katie didn't just win—she won by a lot! Soon, she wasn't just breaking other people's records—she was breaking her own.

In 2015, Katie graduated high school. That same year, she also won every single freestyle race at the World Championships. No one had ever done that before. People called it the Ledecky Slam!

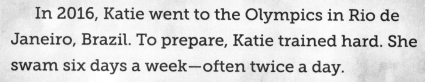

In 2016, Katie went to the Olympics in Rio de Janeiro, Brazil. To prepare, Katie trained hard. She swam six days a week—often twice a day.

Katie again won the 800-meter freestyle race. This time, she beat her own world record by almost twelve seconds! Katie left Rio with four more gold medals and one silver.

After the Rio Olympics, Katie went to Stanford University in California and swam on the college team.

In 2021, she graduated with a degree in psychology. But Katie wasn't on campus for her graduation. She was over a thousand miles away in Omaha, Nebraska—getting ready for the next Olympics.

That summer, Katie won two more gold medals and two silver medals at the Olympics in Tokyo, Japan.

More than ten years after she surprised the world at the London Olympics, Katie is still going strong. In July 2023, she won the 800-meter freestyle at the World Aquatic Championships and became the first swimmer in history to win the same world championship event six years in a row.

Katie has no plans to slow down. She continues to set goals for herself—and swimming at the 2024 Paris Olympics is one of them.

Katie Ledecky is one of the most celebrated athletes of all time. She is a historymaker and a legend. Today she is still dominating her sport, setting new records, and inspiring others.

What's Katie's advice to kids?
"Anything is possible," she says, "so keep working hard and follow your dreams!"